Twenty-Two Signs that You're Called to Be a Prophet

Matthew Robert Payne

This book is copyrighted by Matthew Robert Payne. Copyright © 2018. All rights reserved.

Any part of this book can be photocopied, stored, or shared with anyone for the purposes of encouraging people. You are free to quote this book, use whole chapters of this book on blog posts, or use this book for any reason if it is to spread the message of Jesus with this world. No consent from the author is required of you.

Please visit http://personal-prophecy-today.com to sow into Matthew's writing ministry, to request a personal prophecy or life coaching, or to contact him.

Cover designed by akira007 at fiverr.com

Edited by Lisa Thompson at www.writebylisa.com You can email Lisa at writebylisa@gmail.com for your editing needs.

All scripture is taken from the New King James Version unless otherwise indicated. Copyright © 1982 by Thomas Nelson, Inc. Used by permission. All rights reserved.

Scripture quotations marked (NLT) are taken from the Holy Bible, New Living Translation, copyright ©1996, 2004, 2007, 2013, 2015 by Tyndale House Foundation. Used by permission of Tyndale House Publishers, Inc., Carol Stream, Illinois 60188. All rights reserved.

The opinions expressed by the author are not necessarily those of Christian Book Publishing USA.

Published by Christian Book Publishing USA.

Christian Book Publishing USA is committed to excellence in the publishing industry. Book design Copyright © 2018 by Christian Book Publishing USA. All rights reserved.

Paperback: 978-1-68411-560-0

Hardcover: 978-1-68411-561-7

Dedication

To my mentor and friend:

I want to thank you, Jesus, for letting me come to know you as a young boy of eight years of age. You have been there for me all through my life, staying close even when I walked away from you.

Many people say that a prophet in training needs a prophet to mentor him or her though all I had in my walk was you. I am living proof that a person can be mentored directly by you.

We have shared many highs and lows together. You have been close to me and a very dear friend—sometimes, my only friend. You have shown me many great things and opened up the heavens over my life. In recent years, you have been sending saints from heaven to speak with me, and they have become my friends also.

I long for you. I am hungry for you. I dedicate this book to you, the great apostle of God and prophet who died for me. You are my life.

Acknowledgments

Jesus:
    I know I dedicated this book to you, but I want to thank you for training me to be a prophet and a teacher to the Body of Christ. You use me and bring me so much joy as I live out my life on earth.

Holy Spirit:
    I want to thank you for leading and teaching me. You are a great teacher, better than I could ever be. I want to thank you for speaking through me and being my co-author. I am getting to know you more and more each year.

Father:
    Thank you for loving me and entrusting me with this life that I am living. Thank you for revealing my purpose to me and leading me toward accomplishing it. Thank you so much for your Son, Jesus. Thank you for everything that you have done in my life.

Bethany:
    I want to thank you, Bethany, my scribe angel, for helping me with this book. I certainly felt you as I wrote this book. I saw you dancing in church today as we worshipped. Thank you for being an integral part of my life and purpose.

Lisa Thompson:
    I want to give special thanks to Lisa for copy editing this book of mine. You take my simple words and transform them to make me seem smarter than I really am. If you have any editing needs, Lisa can be contacted at writebylisa@gmail.com

Nicola:
    I want to thank Nicola for being part of my team as a proofreader. I want to thank you for all the work that you did with this book to polish and improve it.

Bill Vincent:
I want to thank you, Bill, for publishing my book. You can contact Revival Waves of Glory Books & Publishing if you need any books published.

Other prophets:
I want to thank all the prophets who have impacted my life over the years. I want to thank you for writing your books and educating me. I think equipping the body and sharing your knowledge in books and videos is vital.

Friends:
I want to thank Lisa, Nicola, Mary, Wendy, Laura, David Joseph, and Michael Van Vlymen for your friendship and how you have impacted my life.

Mom and Dad:
I want to thank my mother and father for all the love that they have given me. I am a product of your love.

Readers and ministry supporters:
I want to thank the readers of my books and my ministry supporters for the income that you have given me to publish books. I live to educate people, and I thank both my readers and the supporters of my ministry because you make life worth living.

Table of Contents

Dedication..3
Acknowledgments 4
Introduction 12
A Prophetic Word...13
Sign 1: You have always felt called 16
    You read the books of the prophets, and your spirit is stirred...16
    You know a few prophets, and you identify with them. 16
    You feel called to the church...17
    You have a desire to bring change for the better to the church. 18
Sign 2: People have prophesied that you are a prophet..................19
    Prophetic people have prophesied over you that you are called to be a prophet. 19
    You have a deep sense that the prophets are right.....................20
Sign 3: You are different from others..22
    You have a hunger for the Christian faith. 22
    You are thirsty..22
    You can't find enough Christian activities. 23
    You can't stop talking about Jesus. 23
    You spend hours reading. 24
    You spend hours watching YouTube. 24
    Money is not an issue for you when it comes to God. 24
Sign 4: The Word is alive to you..26
    You read verses, and they jump off the page. 26
    Scriptures haunt you, and you can't stop thinking about them. 26
    Scriptures mean so much more to you, and you have a deep love for God's Word...27

You have hundreds of questions about scripture and are always seeking more information in the books you read and the videos you watch. 27

You have spent many hours in the Word of God. 28

Sign 5: You are like a deep river. 29

You find it hard to chat about surface issues. 29

You see the story behind the news. 29

You research deeply into subjects that interest you. 30

You think nothing of investing time on research. 30

You can come up with some profound insights. 31

Sign 6: You can be prone to depression. 32

You sometimes become very depressed..................................32

You may have clinical depression and need medication...........33

You feel the sadness of God for the world. 33

The state of the Church disturbs and discourages you. 33

You are sad if you aren't used effectively................................34

Sign 7: You have mood swings of highs and lows. 35

You can become very high and feel anointed. 35

You can have mountain-top experiences...................................35

You can also go into deep ruts and struggle with depression. ..36

Sign 8: You see the spiritual meanings in ordinary things............37

Part 1: The Gift of Discerning of Spirits 37

Part 2: The Gift of Discerning of Spirits 37

You can be typing a document to music playing in the background and type a word at the same time as the same word is sung in the song you are listening to. 38

You see a message on a street sign about stopping, going back, moving forward, slowing down, and so forth. The sign gives you specific direction for your spiritual life as well........................38

You view advertisements in the same way as street signs; they have prophetic messages or confirmation for you. 39

Songs on the radio have a message from God or a confirmation. 39

Love songs might be Jesus singing to you. 40

Sign 9: You respect the Word. 41

You have great regard for the Word of God. 41

Everything you do is founded on the Word. 41

Through the Word, you have come to know the character of God and Jesus. 42

You might have a love of the prophetic books. 43

Sign 10: You have a deep love for God. 44

As you have matured, you have come to know God well. 44

You know God isn't angry, but he is holy. 45

You desire to please God in all you do. 46

You are thankful to God for your life even if it has been hard. 46

Sign 11: You have a deep love for Jesus. 47

You have come to know Jesus through reading the Gospels. ... 47

You are thankful for Jesus's death for you. 47

You may have a deep love for Jesus for what he has done in your life. 48

You talk to Jesus, and he talks back to you. 49

Sign 12: You have a deep love for the Holy Spirit. 50

You recognize the Holy Spirit's role in your life. 50

You are led by the Holy Spirit. 51

You love how the Holy Spirit leads you. 52

Sign 13: The gift of prophecy flows easily through you. 54

Flowing in prophecy comes easily to you. 54

    You are skilled in the three gifts of prophecy: word of knowledge, word of wisdom, and prophecy. 55

    You are always looking to improve, and you are watching other prophets. 56

    You may consume many books on the prophetic. 56

    You are always learning more. 57

Sign 14: You are spiritually hungry. 58

    You have hundreds of questions about the faith and your role. 58

    Every time a question is answered, more questions come up. ... 58

    Your whole life is consumed with the knowledge of God. 59

    The more you learn, the more excited and the hungrier you'll become. 59

Sign 15: You hate sin. 61

    You have grace for sinners, but you don't like sin. 61

    Your posts on social media sometimes address sin. 62

    You are very aware of sin in your own life. 62

Sign 16: You don't like to hear error taught. 64

    It annoys you to hear error taught. 64

    You try to correct error with grace and humility when you can. 65

    You have learned the truth and are a vocal preacher of truth and exposing the error you used to embrace. 65

    You understand that people need to know the truth. 66

    You know that when you have a bigger platform, you will do more in this area. 66

Sign 17: You deal with lots of warfare. 67

    You struggle with a lot of warfare through people that come against you. 67

    Jezebel might come against you many times. 68

    You can go from one hard situation to the next more often than other people. 69

Sign 18: You have a fire in your belly. 70

    You have a message of change for your local church. 70

    You flow and preach from the new wine. 71

    You need to preach a message of love, purity, and holiness. 72

    You want the church to wake up and to stop being lukewarm. .. 72

    You want the platform so that you can share this burden from your heart. 72

Sign 19: You live a supernatural life filled with visions, dreams, and angels. 74

    You hear the Godhead speak to you. 74

    You have the ability to see in the Spirit. 75

    You have prophetic dreams. 75

    You may see angels. 76

    You have been to heaven. 76

    You have met Jesus. 77

    You have met saints 77

Sign 20: You develop the mind of Christ. 79

    Through understanding Christ's teachings and obeying them, you develop the ability to think like Jesus. 79

    You feel the heart of Jesus for people. 80

    You know how Jesus loves a person. 80

    You start to move from knowledge of scripture to wisdom and application of the Word. 80

    You take every thought captive and pull down thoughts that don't agree with the Word of God. 81

Sign 21: You have God's heart. 83

    You have a sense of how God feels. 83

> You can have the heart of God and make decisions based on that intuition and feeling. 84
>
> You love people like God does with grace and compassion. 85

Sign 22: You can be misunderstood and rejected. 86

> Because you are so turned on to Jesus and holy living, you can be brash in your immaturity, which causes people to reject you. 86
>
> You are different. Because you have unique revelation that differs from what has been traditionally taught, you are misunderstood and rejected. 87
>
> You can feel like a square peg in a round hole. 88
>
> People that are closest to you might not accept that you are called to be a prophet. 88
>
> The call to be a prophet takes fifteen to twenty years to develop. If you allow it to, this season of misunderstanding and rejection will mature you into a great prophet. 89

Closing Thoughts 90

I'd love to hear from you.. 93

How to Sponsor a Book Project 94

Other Books by Matthew Robert Payne... 95

About Matthew Robert Payne 98

Introduction

I am happy to see that you are reading this book. You might have the gift of prophecy and have been operating in it for a while. You might wonder if you are actually called to be a prophet.

You can relax; you are in good hands with me. I have been where you are right now. I have been new to the prophetic with many questions. I have been a beginner in the journey toward the office of prophet, and so I understand a little bit of what you might be feeling.

I have invested God's resources into this book because I feel that this subject is much needed. There don't seem to be many people out there helping prophets come to grips with their calling. I hope that as you read this, you can feel my heart.

I would say that the most important signs out of the twenty-two points are sign two and sign twenty-two. If you have been used to rejection all of your life and if people have prophesied that you are called to be a prophet, then you are likely destined to be a prophet.

You might have fifteen to twenty of these signs and still not have the calling of prophet. These signs can be seen in many passionate Christian's lives. If you have many of the signs, I am not saying that you are a prophet. But if you have sign two and twenty-two, you likely are a prophet.

I hope you enjoy my book.

Love,

Matthew Robert Payne

April 2018

A Prophetic Word

Disclaimer: This prophetic word was edited for minor grammar corrections only and was published with the permission of the author and printed as it was received.

"A Prophet Wears the Coat of Many Colors with Humility"

By Prophetess Kelly Turner

As a prophet, you must learn to hold your peace even when you know a person has done you wrong. This is especially difficult to do when it's someone you are very close to. Many people think that prophets don't hurt or experience rejection, mocking, slander, character assassination, and so on.

When you know you're giving another person the benefit of the doubt, and then years later, they turn around and hurt you even more deeply than before, it takes serious humility and, most of all, forgiveness to refrain from speaking from a place of emotion.

Whenever you're attacked and/or ridiculed for hearing and doing the work of the ministry, sometimes it's better to lay low and just let it pass. There will always be that one person that envies the work of a servant's hand. Nothing you have done has caused the person to envy you. Many of you are like Joseph, whose brothers despised the coat of many colors given to him by his father.

I hear the Lord saying, "I'm doing the same for you. I've given you many talents and giftings, and many of your family members feel as though they were supposed to be the one given the honor and not you. But one thing about *me*—I give to whom I choose and know they will not steal *my glory*. When you walk through the desert storm and understand the scorching heat and wind, you know what it's like to be the castaway, and yet you choose love in spite of the opposition. You also know what it's like to be thrown under the bus time and time again because of who I called you to be. Yet you continue to forgive as I tell you to—over and over again. See, this is why I can use you in the capacity that I do. Because the heart you have is the heart of the *king*. There will always be those who hate and despise you because they feel as though they deserve your spot in God's kingdom, but that's not how it happens. You secure your spot according to the pruning, stripping, pressing, and going through the furnace when the heat has reached its maximum capacity. Through the fire, one is tried and tested. There is no room for murmuring and complaining. That's why I use you to the capacity that I do—because of your heart, the hidden heart that no one except *me* sees.

"Many have gone to the best seminary schools, but when I teach you, there is a changing of the guards. I taught you, not man. That's why many wonder, 'How can this be?'

"For didn't I say that by *my* hand, I shall breathe upon a thing, and it shall be? I have breathed upon your life, and now you're transforming into the butterfly I called you to be. You're walking in the fullness of who I created others to see. Let man think they're stealing from you. In reality, they are elevating you to achieve what I already designed to take place.

"I never create something and fail to bring it into fruition. What makes you think I won't fulfill everything that I promised you? I mean everything that I say. You must continue to be an example and love others unconditionally. There will be bumps and bruises and even scabs that will fall off, but you have the heart of the Father, free from infection. Some things have been a big test for you. These things caused you to rehash some old thoughts, memories, and hurts. But in the end, you continue to choose forgiveness and love. For this reason, you've just been promoted again in *my* kingdom."

Prophetess Kelly Turner
Kelly Turner Ministries
http://onbrokenpiecesministries.com/staff/kelly-turner

Sign 1:
You have always felt called

You read the books of the prophets, and your spirit is stirred.

When you've read the Bible, especially Isaiah, Ezekiel, Jeremiah, and the minor prophets, your spirit is stirred. If your whole heart starts to move and you feel your spirit stirring when you read these prophetic biblical books, you might possibly be called as a prophet.

Isaiah is my favorite book in the Bible. This was true before I even knew that I was a prophet. The Gospel of Matthew was my second favorite book, not because of my name, Matthew, but because I definitely love the parables and the stories that Jesus tells in the book of Matthew. Three signposts that you might be called as a prophet follow: 1) if the books of Isaiah, Jeremiah, and the prophets stir your heart, 2) if you have an understanding of God in those books, and 3) if you can relate to and connect with those books.

You know a few prophets, and you identify with them.

You might have watched YouTube and seen some prophets speaking and preaching. As you've watched them, you have felt that you're similar to them. A lot of the things that you say, a lot of the things that you feel and share with people, are similar. These prophets are coming out with the same ideas, the same sentences, the same subjects, and the same revelation that you've been sharing with your friends or that you've been feeling deeply inside.

You can have an understanding of what a prophet is by watching YouTube clips and videos of prophets ministering, preaching, and teaching on the internet. You might easily form an opinion that "This is what I'd like to do. This is the calling that is on my life." You might have this real yearning in your heart to preach and a burning desire in your heart to bring the same sort of message and touch people's lives in the same way as these prophets.

It would not be strange for you to read the scriptures and receive the same sort of revelations that some of these prophets have, the same ideas, and the same teachings that they are sharing. If that's you and if prophets on the internet are sharing what you already know or what you inherently feel through the reading of the scriptures, take that as a sign that you might be called as a prophet. If you are looking at life and looking at the world and at the state of the church, if the prophets are saying similar things as you, you might be called as a prophet. If you'd like to say some things on YouTube in addition to posting on your own Facebook wall, you might be called to be a prophet.

You feel called to the church.

If someone shared with you what an evangelist was, you might feel that although you love people who aren't saved, you don't necessarily feel called to these folks. You might feel a calling to a church, but you might feel that you aren't to pastor a church. Even so, you feel that you have an important message for the Body of Christ. If you feel called to the church, then you might be called to be a prophet.

It's a strange thing. I remember feeling a calling on my life when I was a young boy. I originally thought that I was called to be an evangelist. I felt this real call that God would use me full time.

I heard that a famous evangelist was asked, "How do you know if you're called to be a preacher?" The evangelist said that if you're called to be a preacher, then you won't be happy in any other job.

The evangelist asked, "What do you do?"

The person responded, "I'm a mechanic."

The evangelist asked, "Are you happy being a mechanic?"

The person said, "Yes, I am."

The evangelist said, "Well, you're not called to be a preacher. If you were called to be a preacher, you wouldn't be happy unless you were a preacher."

The same thing happens with the calling on a person's life. When you have a calling on your life, when you feel that you've been called to serve God, then you won't be happy until you are serving God. If you're called to be a prophet, you probably have a message that you want to share with the church. One practical way to start to share that message is to borrow or buy yourself a camera or set up a video from your laptop and start to record YouTube videos. I made over a thousand YouTube videos and taught on a lot of things before I was accepted and invited to speak in church.

You have a desire to bring change for the better to the church.

If you're called to be a prophet, you have a message for the church that will reinvigorate the church. It will give the church an extra boost, an exciting boost for them to go on and be powerful and labor effectively. You'll have revelation and inspiration on how to give an encouraging message to the church to help them become better at what they do.

If all you have is doom-and-gloom messages for the church, then you have a wrong understanding of what you're called to be and what a prophet does. Prophets can have hard messages, but they structure their messages in a way that's very encouraging and hopefully building up the church.

Sign 2:
People have prophesied that you are a prophet.

Prophetic people have prophesied over you that you are called to be a prophet.

When you have the calling of a prophet on your life, there's a strong chance that you'll start to prophesy and mix with people who are prophetic in nature. You can join Facebook groups where people prophesy over each other. Prophetic people in those groups can actually see the calling in you and prophesy that you're called to be a prophet. That's one way that you'll know that you're called as a prophet.

Many people are prophetic or gifted with the gift of prophecy, but they're not prophets. For example, the ability to teach the Word of God doesn't make you a pastor nor does being able to fix your engine make you a mechanic. The person who starts medical school isn't immediately qualified to be a doctor or a surgeon.

A person who merely prophesies can be called prophetic, which is a start. But the office of prophet is something entirely different and takes a lot of years and a lot of maturity.

Prophetic people, those with the gift of prophecy, could prophesy over you that you're called to be a prophet. But if you ever have the opportunity to meet a prophet, someone in the office of a prophet who's recognized as a prophet, and he prophesies over you that you're called to be a prophet, you have just received strong and sure confirmation of your calling.

Please understand that between the time when a prophetic person or a prophet says that you're called to be a prophet and the time when you're actually sitting in the office of a prophet could take anywhere from ten to twenty years. A lot of preparation goes into the life of a prophet to mature him or her into the office of prophet.

A known prophet could prophesy over you that you're called to be a prophet. From that time on, you might understand this prophetic calling. You'll eventually be a prophet, but it will take many years of discipline and training by the Lord for you to be raised up and matured. This process can move along if a prophet takes you under his wing and decides to mentor you. That's always an encouraging way to develop into a prophet.

You have a deep sense that the prophets are right.

When I say prophets there, I mean the prophetic people and those in the office of prophet. If prophetic people prophesy over you and say that you're a prophet called to the nations or that you have the calling of a prophet, you can understand and accept what they say. If a recognized prophet in his office prophesies over you that you're called to be a prophet, this provides further confirmation of your calling. When you have a sense that they are right, then you're on your way to developing your life as a prophet.

Please remember, like I've said, that it will take ten to twenty years for you to become a prophet. You might have the gift of prophecy and be able to move in this gift. You might even be fluent in the gift of prophecy, but you have to prophesy for up to twenty years before God will trust you in the actual office of the prophet.

The calling of a prophet is a hard and difficult calling and a challenging position. If you have patience and endurance, you can persevere for as long as it takes to mature into a prophet and successfully move into the role of a prophet yourself.

One of the things that I found in my life was that the enemy comes against you in your own mind when you think about being a prophet. You might think that you only need to be told by a prophet once that you're called to be a prophet, but it seemed as if I needed to be called or prophesied over about twenty times before I finally started to believe that I was actually called as a prophet.

Even though I felt a calling on my life, even though I felt called to the church, and even though I knew I was called to be a prophet, it took that many people prophesying over me to cement that call in my mind so that I was secure in the knowledge of my calling. This sums up the second point. One of the signs that you're called to be a prophet is that prophetic people will prophesy over you.

Sign 3:
You are different from others.

You have a hunger for the Christian faith.

As someone called to be a prophet, you have a real hunger for everything related to Christianity. You'll have a hunger for the Word, a hunger to read about related topics, and a hunger for these types of materials.

You will constantly have questions and will seek to learn more. You'll be different and weird. People might not understand where you're coming from. You will have this insatiable hunger and thirst for God.

You are thirsty.

Once again, you have a thirst for all things related to God. It seems that no matter how many books you read, no matter how many YouTube videos you watch, no matter how many sermons you hear, you're thirsty for more and more and more. You're a ravenous man or woman, someone who's always thirsty, constantly drinking from the well to fill yourself up. But within hours, you're thirsty again.

You're very different from the majority of Christians who are quite happy just to attend a two-hour service with a half-an-hour sermon per week, and that's it. They don't spend time on YouTube. They don't read articles or books like you do. They're just happy and content to come to church every Sunday, and the Christian faith doesn't consume them.

You can't find enough Christian activities.

If church were every night of the week, if a revival were going on in your church every night, you'd be at church every day after work. You'd go to church and stay until the last people left.

You have this passion, this zeal, and this excitement for everything to do with the Christian life. You have an undeniable thirst and hunger for the Christian faith. You're totally consumed with everything to do with Jesus, God, the Holy Spirit, and angels.

Early in your prophetic life, you attend numerous Christian activities. You won't complain about how much it costs. You go to conferences and read books. You do all sorts of Christian activities to learn more and more about God. You are absolutely consumed with God.

Your whole life spins on an axis of God as if God is your sun, and you rotate around him. Everything that you think about and everything that you do is focused on God—how you can be a servant to him and how you can learn more about him.

You can't stop talking about Jesus.

It's taken real discipline for me to quiet down and speak to people about other topics besides Jesus. I've been on my prophetic journey for over twenty years.

Jesus is my passion. He is everything to me. I have an intensely rich and dynamic relationship with Jesus. People who know me and who've read my thirty-eight books will know that I have a tremendous relationship with Jesus.

When you're called to be a prophet, you cannot stop talking about Jesus. Everything about Jesus and about the Christian faith is on the table to discuss. In fact, you can't handle small talk about sports, TV shows, and other carnal topics. Your hunger and thirst are for Jesus and everything related to him. It's very hard to shift your focus off the Christian faith and life.

You spend hours reading.

Not all prophets are readers, but I imagine that a lot of them are. I certainly am as I have about five hundred books on my Kindle. I have read over half of them. It's taken many years for me to slow down my reading.

As a writer myself, I have to keep fresh. I have to keep reading and continuing to learn, putting more material into my life. If you're called to be a prophet, you might be a voracious reader, someone who reads book after book after book. You not only read books, but you take steps to apply the teachings and the lessons that you learn in the books.

You spend hours watching YouTube.

As someone called to be a prophet who's passionate and thirsty for the things of God, you might watch certain teachers or prophets on YouTube for hundreds of hours. In fact, you need internet plans with unlimited data allowances or at least large allowances so that you can watch all the YouTube videos that interest you.

You don't really worry about how much time you spend reading or watching YouTube. You simply want answers to your questions. You have this unbelievable thirst and hunger for knowledge, and you'll spend time chasing after it.

Money is not an issue for you when it comes to God.

You don't worry about spending money on the following:
- Going to conferences,
- Buying books,
- Your internet connection so that you can watch a lot of YouTube videos,
- Resources for the Christian faith,
- And similar materials that will help you grow.

None of these expenses are an issue to you. You have no problem spending money buying resources so that you can get to know more of God.

It's amazing. You might have a tremendous book collection of spiritual books that you're reading, learning, and gleaning from. You're different. You're totally consumed with Jesus. Jesus is at the top of every one of your conversations, which makes you quite different and weird.

Sign 4:
The Word is alive to you.

You read verses, and they jump off the page.

Many people who are not called as prophets or who don't have a calling on their lives aren't zealous for Jesus. They don't have much of an anointing on their lives. They can read the Bible and be easily bored.

I remember one teacher shared with me that her Muslim husband had trouble sleeping. This preacher said to the Muslim, "Just find a Bible and start to read it every night. You'll be able to go to sleep. Start in Matthew." Sure enough, he started to read the Bible. Every time he read a page, he became very tired and fell asleep. He eventually became a Christian.

That's normally par for the course for many Christians. The Bible is boring and lifeless to them. When you're called to be a prophet—when you're hungry for the Lord and when he is hungry for you—the verses in the Bible tend to jump off the page at you.

So much revelation flows as you read the Word of God. The Holy Spirit speaks back to you and shares his thoughts and influence in your life. The Bible can be incredibly exciting.

Scriptures haunt you, and you can't stop thinking about them.

You might read certain scriptures in the Bible that seem to follow you around. To use a different word, they haunt you. They keep on appearing, turning up in your mind or memory. You might even hear pastors preach on them.

In this way, the Lord is having you meditate on those verses. He's bringing them to your mind time and time again so that you can develop the mind of Christ. You are developing this pattern in your mind that will constantly rely on those verses that keep showing up. When the Lord does that, he's trying to make a pathway in your mind so that you automatically go down that track in certain situations. Your life will conform itself to those scriptures.

Scriptures mean so much more to you, and you have a deep love for God's Word.

You can be totally blown away by some of the scriptures that you read in the Bible. Certain passages of scripture, certain verses, might really stand out to you, such as the ones we just talked about that haunt you. They mean so much more to you than an average Christian. You can talk about a scripture verse to another Christian, and they might wonder why you are so excited about that verse.

Ephesians 3:20 haunted me for about five years. It reads: "Now to Him who is able to do exceedingly abundantly above all that we ask or think, according to the power that works in us."

This verse deeply touched my heart and ministered to me for many years. I meditated on it for a long time, and it means so much to me.

You have hundreds of questions about scripture and are always seeking more information in the books you read and the videos you watch.

You're hungry and thirsty to know the real in-depth meaning of hundreds of verses in the Bible. You don't want just a basic understanding of those verses. You want to know the truth. You want to know what those verses actually mean.

Matthew 7:23, which says "Depart from me, I never knew you," has been on my mind for about fifteen years. To understand the real meaning of what Jesus meant by that, we need to consider who he was talking to. Does this mean that certain people who do signs, wonders, and miracles will go to hell? That's certainly what that scripture seems to indicate.

You have hundreds of questions. You want to know the meaning of hundreds of scriptures. As you read books, watch videos, listen to sermons, and go to conferences, you'll constantly be on the lookout for a teacher that can bring you revelation on those verses that you have questions about.

You have spent many hours in the Word of God.

You meditate on the Word of God day and night. Psalm 1 speaks about that with a wonderful promise.

Psalm 1:1–3 says, "Blessed is the man who walks not in the counsel of the ungodly, nor stands in the path of sinners, nor sits in the seat of the scornful; but his delight *is* in the law of the Lord, and in His law he meditates day and night. He shall be like a tree planted by the rivers of water, that brings forth its fruit in its season, whose leaf also shall not wither; and whatever he does shall prosper."

Your life will be like a tree planted by the rivers that gives fruit in the proper season, and your leaf will not wither. Nothing will happen to derail you in hard times, difficult times, or years of drought. You'll always have an abundance of fruit in your life. Whatever you do shall prosper.

A person who lives, breathes, and meditates on the Word of God day and night has a life full of spiritual fruit that isn't affected by seasons or economics. Whatever you do will prosper. That person is walking out scripture. That person is often going over scripture and spending many hours in the Word of God: meditating on it, chewing on it, and living their life according to it.

The Word is alive to you. You don't just know or quote the Word of God, but the Word of God is living in you and is being fashioned in you. You're actually living out the Word of God. You will live out many of the verses in the Bible in a practical and daily way if you're called to be a prophet.

Sign 5:
You are like a deep river.

You find it hard to chat about surface issues.

If you have the calling of a prophet on your life, you might find it hard to talk about the weather, the news, football, sports, or other daily subjects. Your subject is Jesus and his kingdom. You are totally malnourished when people are talking about inconsequential topics.

You have a passion for Jesus, his kingdom, and everything related to the kingdom. You really want to focus on that and talk about it. You want to mix with people who want to talk about Jesus and who are active in pursuing Jesus just like you are.

You see the story behind the news.

As a prophet, you can be watching the news, and you can see the reason behind why reporters are saying what they say or how they're reporting the news. You can know the reason and the agenda of the reporters as they report.

You can see the story behind the news and the related agenda just like the agenda at the moment in the media or in the West, in America, or in Australia is to criticize and pull down everything Donald Trump is doing. You see the agenda of the media—they want the Democrats to be in power, and they just cannot stand Donald Trump and his presidency.

You see the story behind the news. It affects you and makes you emotional. I don't even watch the news in Australia because, whenever they talk about Donald Trump, I almost feel like jumping through the TV screen, grabbing the person, and giving him a piece of my mind. As a prophet, I rarely watch the news, but sometimes when I do watch it, I can have a conversation with Jesus about the reasons why different things are happening.

You research deeply into subjects that interest you.

If you're called to be a prophet, you research deeply into subjects that interest you. You don't just do a surface investigation, but you plunge into the depths of a subject.

You're like a submarine. You don't remain on the surface, but most of your time is spent in the deep waters because that's where Jesus is.

In all that you research, you plunge the depths of your Christian faith, the depths of knowledge and wisdom with everything that you do. You're passionate about the kingdom and about everything related to Jesus.

You spend time researching what you consider. You spend copious amounts of time reading and watching YouTube videos. Even when you watch news broadcasts, you watch other perspectives on YouTube by choice instead of depending on what the media feeds you. If you are political, you'll seek out the right commentators that back Trump, and you listen to everything they have to say.

You think nothing of investing time on research.

You spend hours and hours watching Christian videos or videos by a certain prophet that you love. You don't think anything of investing time into research. You can spend one hundred hours watching most of Kat Kerr's teachings because you enjoy the supernatural and the subject of heaven.

You're not at all fazed or worried about the huge investment of time that you put into studying these subjects. You're hungry and thirsty for more. Time isn't an issue to you.

Many people think you're weird because of that. Many people think that the amount of time you spend on YouTube rather than watching normal TV makes you strange and difficult to deal with. But people can think about you that way because you're tuned to a different frequency that is not of this world.

You're not attracted to the things of the world, the lust, or the pleasures of the world. You're attracted to the kingdom of God and his love in your life. You'll do anything to know more about that kingdom and to progress in your spiritual walk.

You can come up with some profound insights.

Sometimes when you post on Facebook or when you're conversing with people, you say something that is very deep, profound, and rich. It comes naturally to you. You have applied knowledge that you gained through research and put it into practice. In this way, you've learned to walk in wisdom.

The Holy Spirit said to me ten years ago that wisdom is the proper application of knowledge. That's a profound and true statement. The world contains so much knowledge, many books, and YouTube videos on all kinds of subjects in the Christian faith. But very few Christians are applying that knowledge. They listen and research, but they don't apply what they learn.

When you're applying the knowledge, you can come up with some pretty profound insights. You are used to walking with Jesus, hand in hand with him, talking to him, and learning about him and his kingdom. That's just the wisdom of God operating in you. When you speak these profound insights, people will sometimes think you're weird and different. On the other hand, some people might think for a whole year and couldn't come up with one of your Facebook posts.

People can become jealous of you and envy you because you post such amazing things on Facebook. That's another sign that you run deep.

Sign 6:
You can be prone to depression.

You sometimes become very depressed.

We live in a world that seems to struggle with depression, which can discourage you at times. When you're used to operating and moving by the Spirit of God and being directed by him, the sheer carnal nature of man and hopelessness of the world can weigh you down and bother you. Sometimes you actually might find yourself feeling depressed.

We can see that Jeremiah and other prophets became depressed. King David dealt with depression. In one of his writings, Jeremiah wished that he'd never been born. In one of the psalms, David wept on his pillow the whole night. Depression happens to anointed people. It's just part of warfare from the enemy.

Don't be ashamed to admit that sometimes you become depressed and succumb to depression. That can just be another sign that you're called to be a prophet. Some people label that type of personality as melancholy.

I suffered from a mental illness for many years, a bipolar condition. I'm mostly healed now. I went to a ministry called Freedom Encounters at the following link: https://www.freedomencounters.com I went through deliverance with them a couple of years ago and am thankful that I haven't dealt with serious depression since. But it is true that I used to become quite depressed.

You may have clinical depression and need medication.

Don't be afraid of going to a doctor or taking medication for depression. It's not a failure on your part or on God's part. Of course, faith can make you well, and you can receive healing. If you become clinically depressed or suicidal, you should probably see a doctor for medication to help stabilize you again.

When you're called to be a prophet, the enemy is angry and upset. When he sees you headed toward your destiny, he has some idea of what your destiny is. He has often heard the prophetic words over your life, and he becomes upset. He wants to stop you from reaching your destiny.

If he can send you into a cycle of depression or even put clinical depression on you, he will be happy. He's the thief that wants to rob, kill, and destroy your life. He'll do anything to stop you, pull you back, and give you a hard time. Don't be afraid of taking medication.

The sign of depression might be true of all prophets. It might just be relevant to this personality. It was relevant to me until a couple of years ago. This can certainly be a sign that you're called as a prophet.

You feel the sadness of God for the world.

Some of the sadness and burdens in my own life are because I feel the very heart of God for this world. I feel his emotions. I feel how he feels about the slave trade, international trafficking, sexual abuse, and all those horrific crimes against humanity. I feel his heart. In that way, I feel the sadness of the Lord, which can be depressing.

The state of the Church disturbs and discourages you.

If called as a prophet, you might understand through scripture what the state of the church should look like. You can understand it through reading the Gospel of Acts and understanding what happened in the early church. Paul was clear about what the standard of church should be.

You can see through the scriptures that the modern church falls short of that standard, which can discourage you. Some churches are preaching a doctrine of grace so extreme that crazy things happen, which depresses and upsets you. They even deny that hell exists and deny the rapture. All sorts of things happen in the church that have caused people to go astray. The state of the church disturbs and discourages you so that you feel sad. Looking at the state of the church can lead to sadness and depression in your life.

You are sad if you aren't used effectively.

One thing that can really discourage you if you have a calling on your life is waiting until you're used—waiting for a chance to speak in a pulpit, waiting for a chance to minister, or waiting for an open door to use your gifts. It can be a long and hard wait.

You might feel like you were put on a shelf and forgotten. You don't feel like you're part of the team. You feel as if you have been put on the bench for a whole season, and you don't even get to play in one game.

You want to play and be in the field in the middle of the action. You want to be ministering and teaching people, and yet you're held back. These long years, ten or twenty years of waiting to release what's in your heart, waiting to have a platform, can be depressing and get you down.

I wanted to make these points about being sad and being depressed. These are some of the reasons why I have been depressed. You could become depressed and discouraged for many other reasons when you're called to be a prophet.

Sign 7:
You have mood swings of highs and lows.

You can become very high and feel anointed.

I'm not sure about you, and I don't know where you're coming from. I don't know everything about you, but I can put on worship music and get in a spiritual high. I can feel the anointing and the joy and the peace of the Lord, walking in his presence. My spirit can become high, like ecstasy, a very happy, joyful, and peaceful state of being.

The presence of the Lord allows that. Years ago, people called these mountain-top experiences where you might have received a new revelation of the Bible. You might have a new insight into the Bible that you haven't heard taught or preached before. The revelation, this insight and new knowledge, can give you a spiritual high.

You can come to a place where you truly feel good, happy, and blessed. You feel as though you can conquer the world. You might reach this place if you are called to the prophetic.

You can have mountain-top experiences.

Like I just said, you can have these mountain-top experiences. The air seems thin; the veil between heaven and earth is thin. You might have visions, angelic experiences, and meet and talk with Jesus. You might go to heaven and live under an open heaven with this tremendous, joyful experience if you are called as a prophet.

These experiences should be part of your life and are valuable to every Christian. I guess that's one of the reasons why people go to conferences and to many events in the Christian church—to get a spiritual high, to get a buzz.

I know of one major church in Sydney that has a conference every year. You feel like you're on cloud nine for the week of the conference. It's just at another level. So I imagine that many Christians go to conferences to feel that spiritual buzz.

You can also go into deep ruts and struggle with depression.

Like we covered in the previous point, you can go into states of depression as a prophet for various reasons. The last section was all about depression because I felt I needed to address it. If you are called to the prophetic, you can go from the highest highs to the lowest lows. So you might be on a spiritual high from going to a conference for a week and then a couple of days after you return, you feel low, sad, and depressed.

You can go through these mood fluctuations, depending how often you go to conferences or to events. You can experience this roller coaster of highs and lows, and you can actually settle into that as a part of your life, flowing from the lowest lows to very high highs.

I have suffered for many years with bipolar disorder and the related highs and lows. I know that many people who are called to the prophetic office or who are called as a future prophet also struggle in similar ways.

I mentioned this point so that you understand what you are facing is not uncommon if you're going through these various fluctuations of highs and lows. In fact, people who are called into the prophetic commonly go through this. The Lord loves it when you have your highs, but he doesn't necessarily love it when you have your lows. Sure, the enemy likes you to experience your lows, but that seems to be common for so many people. You might want to become used to this and almost accept it as a part of your life and how you will live out your calling as a prophet.

Sign 8:
You see the spiritual meanings in ordinary things.

Jennifer Eivaz, a prophet, has a couple of forty-five-minute videos that I have linked here. If you are reading the paperback version of this book, you can search for the videos on YouTube by typing in the title I have listed. If you are on Kindle, I suggest that you go to the link and listen to these videos.

Part 1: The Gift of Discerning of Spirits

https://www.youtube.com/watch?v=2kgZtjFLPbk&t=311s

Part 2: The Gift of Discerning of Spirits

https://www.youtube.com/watch?v=eR65Dw3mrCo&t=1030s

She talks about the gift of discerning of spirits. It's not just a gift of discerning evil spirits or evil people. But this gift encompasses a whole different range of things. I'll be talking about some of the different ways you can discern spirits in this segment.

I strongly recommend that you go to these links and listen to these videos because if you think you're weak, strange, way out there, and that you don't fit in with other people that you know, you'll find a lot of comfort in these videos. They explain this topic a whole lot better than what I will do in this section.

You can be typing a document to music playing in the background and type a word at the same time as the same word is sung in the song you are listening to.

One way that God confirms things for me is that I might be on Facebook posting a post with some worship music playing in the background. Then this happens: At the same time that I'm typing something, the same word is playing on the worship music. In this way, I know that what I'm posting is anointed or what I've written in one of my books is anointed.

God does that so often with me. He must strongly motivate me to play certain songs at certain times because he knows that my manuscript has a specific place with that word. At the same time, the song plays the same words as what's being read. I call this a form of synchronicity. If a person isn't prophetic, that probably wouldn't mean much. They might not even notice or think that it was special. But someone called to the prophetic can see that this has a spiritual meaning and purpose to encourage them.

You see a message on a street sign about stopping, going back, moving forward, slowing down, and so forth. The sign gives you specific direction for your spiritual life as well.

You can be on the road—walking, in a bus, or in a car—and you can see a street sign with some type of message. For example, the sign says "wrong way, go back." You know that you need to turn your car around and to not proceed.

While the sign means something in the natural, it also means something in the spiritual. You might have made a decision to start or to publish a book, or you might have made a decision to leave your church. Whatever the decision, that sign can have a spiritual emphasis to it and can be anointed the moment you read it. It can give you direction about changing a decision that you just made about what you will do. You might need to turn around, go back, and change your decision.

You view advertisements in the same way as street signs; they have prophetic messages or confirmation for you.

You might be worried about something: finances, a job, or your child, and God has been telling you in your spirit when you talk to him, "Don't worry. Take one day at a time."

You might have been fairly resistant to God speaking to you that way as you tend to worry. The message of taking one day at a time might not be getting through to you. So one day, you come across an advertisement with a nice picture for a certain product that says "Don't worry; take one day at a time."

The part that says "Don't worry; take one day at a time" really stands out to you because it confirms what God has been telling you. You take it as a spiritual sign to yourself, and you are encouraged by the positive direction and confirmation it gives. Now you know that God is definitely speaking to you.

Songs on the radio have a message from God or a confirmation.

You might have a decision to make. You might be thinking about doing something. The lyrics in the song on the radio when you're in a store or when you're playing the radio at home will play at the same time you're thinking about that decision. The song will confirm the decision that you need to make.

Now to people who aren't spiritually inclined or called to be a prophet, it might seem weird to talk about these things. But someone with the discernment of spirits understands that this is all part of the process.

Some doctors might call all of these signs of schizophrenia because that's how they define spiritual things. They call them mental illnesses. So when you listen to the videos by Jennifer Eivaz, you will realize that a whole new world has opened up to you. Jennifer will explain to you that all these things are part of the gift that God has given you.

Love songs might be Jesus singing to you.

You imagine Jesus singing the love song to you. You can't hear the love song any other way. Whenever you hear that love song, it's as if Jesus is singing to you. You're not crazy; you're just called to be a prophet.

Sign 9:
You respect the Word.

You have great regard for the Word of God.

If you are called to the prophetic office, it is integral and paramount that you have a high regard for the Word of God.

If the Word of God isn't important to you, then the foundation of all you say and do will be on faulty ground. The foundation won't be stable. But if you value the Word and treat it with integrity and honor, then you'll build a solid ministry.

For years, I studied the prophets and the Word of God and read the Bible voraciously. I spent much time in the Word. I put quite a few verses of the Word of God into my spirit. So I can capture every thought that comes into my mind and discern whether the action that stems from the thought agrees with the Word or not. I can decide what actions to take with my life, depending on what the Word of God says.

If you don't respect or know the Word, then you might make decisions and do things that contradict how God wants you to live.

You learn to not only respect the Word as a way to live, but you actually respect the Word in the process of bringing your sermon and bringing a message.

Everything you do is founded on the Word.

Every major decision, every action you take, every view that you hold, and the decisions you make are founded on the Word. I am repeating myself here. I want you to understand that if you start prophesying and speaking something that seems to come from God into other people's lives without a strong foundation in the Word of God, you might be deceived. You might deceive others and lead people astray and do damage to them.

Everything you do as a called prophet should be founded on the Word of God. The Word of God can be twisted and used as a tool to distort people and take people away from the truth. It can be also used to support the truth. When you have a solid understanding of the Word of God in your own personal life, you won't feel the need to always back up everything with the Word of God when you share a message. But your life and everything you do should be founded on the Word of God and what the Bible teaches.

Through the Word, you have come to know the character of God and Jesus.

If you take the time to read Isaiah 40–66, you'll find that God the Father explains himself and life. I am not sure if there is any place more significant in the Bible than those twenty-six chapters to come to know God like you do when you read it.

It's a fascinating insight into God the Father with a crystal-clear picture of who God is. I think it's one of the best collections of verses that you can read to come to understand God.

Through the Word of God, we come to understand who God is and who Jesus is. You need more than the Word of God to understand Jesus. You need to understand what he taught and start to apply it.

The Word of God can be helpful but only if you apply it and make it come alive in your life. You can find the character of God and of Jesus through the Word of God. Of course, preachers can share with you what God and Jesus are like based on their experiences, but the Word of God is powerful.

I have a series of books: <u>*Conversations with God: Book 1*</u>, <u>*Conversations with God: Book 2*</u>, and <u>*Conversations with God: Book 3*</u>. Each of these books will give you an understanding of the character of God as he speaks to me back and forth in a journal form of communication.

I wrote a book called *Finding Intimacy with Jesus Made Simple* and a book called *Jesus Speaking Today*. Those two books will give you an understanding of who Jesus is. But everything in those books is based on the Word of God and the character of God found within the Bible.

You might have a love of the prophetic books.

If you're called to be a prophet, you might have a great love for the books written by the prophets in the Old Testament. Not that you'll become an Old Testament prophet, but you'll certainly be impressed with the prophetic books in the Bible. You'll understand how God used to work and how righteous and merciful God is. You'll find the character of God in the prophetic books.

Sign 10:
You have a deep love for God.

As you have matured, you have come to know God well.

As you read the prophetic books in the Bible, you need to come to realize who God is through the lens of Jesus Christ. If you understand the character of Jesus and that he modeled what the Father was, then you will have a solid foundation to be a modern prophet. Jesus said, "If you've seen me, you've seen the Father" (John 14:9). As you see God through the lens of Jesus and as you come to understand God, who is in Jesus, according to John 17, you come to know God well.

As you come to know God well, you develop a love for him by growing in the prophetic, becoming closer to him, and gaining a deeper understanding of what he is like. You have a better understanding of what he did for you. You build a relationship of trust with him so that you can then obey him.

God shared one thing with me. If we obey God, we come to realize that what he says is right. As we obey what he tells us to do in his commandments and in Jesus's commandments, we come to realize that he is wise. Once we realize that he is wise and works things out for the best when we do it his way, we come to trust him.

The more that we trust God, the more faith we have in him. The more we love God, the more we trust God, and the more we love God, the more we'll obey God. This cycle just spirals upward. The more we obey God, the more we come to realize that he's wise, so we trust him even more. The more we trust him, the more we love him. The more we love him, the more we'll obey him.

Many people say that they love God, but they don't trust him. I'll repeat that. Many people say that they love God, but they don't trust him. It's important to not only say that you love God but that you trust God because, if people trust him, they obey him and walk in his commandments. People need to obey him and apply the promises in the Bible to their lives. Promises in the Bible can help you navigate life, making it richer and fuller. People still live in defeat because they don't trust that God will fulfill his promises in the Bible for them.

As you grow in trust, obedience, and love for God, he fulfills the desires of your heart, and you end up loving him more.

You know God isn't angry, but he is holy.

God is a holy God, and you need to see him as such. He doesn't want anyone to have any gods before him, such as TV, other relationships, or riches. He doesn't want anything to come between you and him, especially when you're called as a prophet.

God respects holiness and righteous living. He calls us to be set apart, to come out of the world, and to forsake the things of the world.1 John 2:15–17 (NLT) says: "Do not love this world nor the things it offers you, for when you love the world, you do not have the love of the Father in you. For the world offers only a craving for physical pleasure, a craving for everything we see, and pride in our achievements and possessions. These are not from the Father, but are from this world. And this world is fading away, along with everything that people crave. But anyone who does what pleases God will live forever."

You will see that this verse says that God doesn't like us going after the things of the world or the things that impress the world.

James 4:4 says, "Adulterers and adulteresses! Do you not know that friendship with the world is enmity with God? Whoever therefore wants to be a friend of the world makes himself an enemy of God."

This verse says that you can't be a lover of the world and a lover of God. If you're a lover of the world, you're an enemy of God. The concept of holiness is not fully understood by people. They think that being holy is just living a sinless life. But being holy actually includes a life that's set apart and devoted to only God with no other gods before him. Nothing in your life is more important than God. He desires you to walk accordingly, and he can become upset if you don't obey him.

You desire to please God in all you do.

If you are called as a prophet, you have a passion and desire to please God in everything you say and do. It doesn't please God for you to call people names or argue on Facebook. You can have a heated discussion on Facebook as long as you're not calling people names, pulling them down, or savagely attacking them.

God doesn't like that. He doesn't mind it when you try to reason with someone on Facebook, but he doesn't want you fighting like a pig in the mud and getting yourself dirty. He wants you to live your life according to how Jesus taught you to live your life in his fifty commandments. If you didn't know that Jesus had fifty commandments, you can click the article title here: <u>The Fifty Commands of Jesus</u>. If you are reading the paperback, you can search for "The Fifty Commands of Jesus."

Jesus wants you to live your life and do everything that these commandments ask you to do if you're a follower of God.

You are thankful to God for your life even if it has been hard.

The life of a prophet can be very hard, but when you're called to be a prophet, you need to reach a point where you're thankful to God for your life. You need to reach a place where you're happy. God is molding you, and you're happy that he has a future for you. You're happy with the prophecies over your life. You're determined to be patient and to let God have his perfect way with you.

Sign 11:
You have a deep love for Jesus.

You have come to know Jesus through reading the Gospels.

The more you read the Gospels, the more you understand Jesus and come to realize who he is. You learn what he was about, and you come to love him.

One way to understand what Jesus taught is to look up the fifty commands of Jesus that he taught us to do as his followers. You can look them up above at the link. I strongly suggest you look these up and paste the article into an MS Word document or similar program. Print out that article and put it on your fridge. Decide to come to know Jesus by obeying him.

Another way to learn to know Jesus is to read the book I've written, _The Parables of Jesus Made Simple: Updated and Expanded Edition_. You can buy it for ninety-nine cents on Kindle. This would give you an understanding of Jesus's teachings in the parables, what he meant, and how to practically live out those parables.

Without an understanding of what Jesus taught and what he meant when he taught certain things, you will not have a deep understanding of him. That will affect your love for him and your ability to serve him in a fuller and more meaningful way to impact the world.

You are thankful for Jesus's death for you.

If you are called to bring change and a radical turnaround to the church, if you will be used to bring reformation or a new wine to the church, you must be thankful for the death of Jesus for you.

It seems that the more you sin, the more you've fallen short in life, and the more Jesus has forgiven you, the more you are thankful for his death and his blood. Mary Magdalene washed Jesus's feet with her hair and tears. Jesus forgave her. He said of Mary Magdalene, one that has been forgiven much, loves much. (See Luke 7:36–50.) I don't know about you, but I have sinned a lot in my life. I have come to fully understand and love Jesus for the price he paid on the cross for my sins.

If you are going to represent God, you might need to take an inventory of your life and realize what Jesus has done for you. Sometimes we become complacent when we're too familiar with someone. Sometimes even in Christian circles, we are not as thankful as we should be. But if you take an honest inventory, if you take some time to actually think of your life and how often Jesus has been there for you, you come to love Jesus even more as you realize all the different ways he's worked in your life and worked out situations for you.

You may have a deep love for Jesus for what he has done in your life.
The more you think about the sins that you've committed and how Jesus has forgiven you, the more you focus on the good things that Jesus has done for you, which will further lead you into a deep love for Jesus. As you come to obey Jesus and understand his parables and his commands, as you start to walk the way Jesus taught, you'll realize that he's wise. You'll learn that following his way is a smart thing to do.

As those things work out the right way for you, you'll realize that you can trust Jesus. The more you trust him, the more you'll love him. The more you love him, the more you'll obey him.

I also said that in the section about the Father, but it bears repeating because, once you understand that, you'll realize that your first step is to obey Jesus. Only when you obey Jesus will you learn how wise he is.

You talk to Jesus, and he talks back to you.

If you have a conversational relationship with Jesus, then it stands to reason that you grow more in love with Jesus as you communicate with him. Jesus is gentle, kind, loving, patient, and faithful. He has so many beautiful characteristics about him. The more you discuss your life, the more he works in your life, leading you, holding your hand, and walking with you through fires.

If you are called as a prophet, you will have a deep love affair with Jesus as you come to love and respect him more. You will cultivate a deep intimacy with him.

Although it's not mentioned as a point, prophetic people regularly speak to and communicate with Jesus. This can even lead to intercession and praying for others. Many prophets are called to be intercessors. Although not all intercessors are prophets, many prophets are intercessors.

When you pray enough, your ability to talk back and forth with Jesus will be a strength in your life. You'll be more and more effective in the Christian life and in your prophetic life when you have a great relationship with Jesus.

Sign 12:
You have a deep love for the Holy Spirit.

You recognize the Holy Spirit's role in your life.

The Holy Spirit has many roles in your life: teaching you, leading you, guiding you, comforting you, and helping you to move in the gifts of the Spirit.

The Holy Spirit is the best interpreter of the Bible, doctor of divinity or any Bible professor. He understands the Word of God better than anyone, even better than Satan.

The Holy Spirit is in your life to lead, direct, and train you to be the prophet that you're called to be. When you recognize that the Holy Spirit is humble, when you realize that he doesn't like to take center stage, when you realize that he wants to empower, bless, lead, guide, and teach you, you'll begin to have a great respect for the Holy Spirit.

I call him the Holy Spirit. Many people just call him Holy Spirit, but I call him *the* Holy Spirit. He's a friend of mine. He puts the very words in my mouth that I speak to dictate a book. He and my scribe angel Bethany inspire everything I have to say.

As I got ready to write this book, I only had the chapter titles and headings for each lesson. What I said wasn't prepared ahead of time. When you don't have preparation notes on the page, this gives the Holy Spirit a lot of room to use your voice and to actually preach the sermons through you rather than you preaching your own sermon.

The Holy Spirit is everything that Jesus said he would be and more. He can be your personal friend. You can talk back and forth with him. You can develop a great love for the Holy Spirit. You can have a great relationship with him.

You are led by the Holy Spirit.

As a prophet in training, you want to develop the ability to be led by the Holy Spirit. Some people act on their intuition. They usually have a feeling to call their mother or to go shopping at a certain time. God can lead them in each of these situations. The Holy Spirit uses their intuition in their thought life to call someone. For example, they might call their mother and learn that she was trying to reach them to talk to them.

These thoughts can be prophetic. God might want you to meet someone at the shopping center, so you feel that you should go shopping at a certain time. The Holy Spirit can lead you to the store at just the right time. You might have a prophetic word for the person at the mall.

You can be led by the Holy Spirit even if you don't have a strong relationship with him. He might command you to go to the mall as he wants you to meet someone. He might tell you to call your mother. He might speak in a clear voice so that you understand that it's the Holy Spirit.

For example, the Holy Spirit will tell me to give some money to Kiva at https://www.kiva.org This website allows you to give money to entrepreneurs in developing countries so that they can start a business. I give quite often there. The Holy Spirit will direct me to give twenty-five or fifty dollars to someone from time to time. He'll direct me to a certain person in need and tell me how much to give to them.

He will direct me to different ministries and tell me what to give. Michael Van Vlymen has written a great book on giving called *Supernatural Provision: Learning to Walk in Greater Levels of Stewardship and Responsibility and Letting Go of Unbiblical Beliefs*. This wonderful book tells you how to give so that God will reward you.

The Holy Spirit can lead and direct you in many other ways and in various levels. Nearly everything I do is led by the Holy Spirit.

You love how the Holy Spirit leads you.

Part of your understanding and the way that you develop your love for the Holy Spirit is by respecting how he leads you through the experiences you have in life that were set up by him. You have learned to deeply love and admire him because he knows best. He knows how to lead and direct you and knows the best outcomes for your life. He knows God's will for your life and how to get you there.

The more you're aware of the Holy Spirit, the more the Holy Spirit directs your paths. Then you're definitely blessed.

Proverbs 3:5–6 says, "Trust in the Lord with all your heart, and lean not on your own understanding; in all your ways acknowledge Him, and He shall direct your paths."

That verse means trust in the Lord with all of your spirit. Trust in the Holy Spirit. Lean not onto your own understanding. Don't be directed by your mind, but be directed by the Holy Spirit through your intuition and your heart. That's what the verse says.

In all of your ways, acknowledge God. Put him first. Do what God tells you to do, and he will make your paths straight. He will direct your paths, and he'll make everything work out fine and dandy.

So many people have confusion in their lives. Their lives don't work out simply because they are not being led by the Holy Spirit, and they are not actively choosing to obey God and do things his way.

Sign 13:
The gift of prophecy flows easily through you.

Flowing in prophecy comes easily to you.

I first started giving prophetic words before I realized that this was prophecy. I've been doing it for years. I used to drive a taxi. Jesus used to tell me to give a certain passenger a message from him, and I would just deliver that message.

Years later, I went to a Pentecostal church and took a course on the spiritual gifts. I realized that there was a name for what I did: the gift of prophecy. If you're called to be a prophet, the gift of prophecy will flow easily through you. Of course, many people are just prophetic and have the gift of prophecy, but they are not called as a prophet.

One of the biggest misconceptions in the Christian world is when people have the gift of prophecy and then assume that they're prophets. I know of one major online training school that never tells people this. They don't warn them that they might not necessarily be a prophet even if they have received the gift of prophecy. They don't tell the students that it might take fifteen to twenty years to become a prophet.

I was very upset about this as it leads to people running around, telling other people that they are prophets just because they have the gift of prophecy. This is not healthy.

When you're called as a prophet, the gift of prophecy flows easily through you.

You are skilled in the three gifts of prophecy: word of knowledge, word of wisdom, and prophecy.

A word of knowledge is past or present information about a person from a supernatural source. You wouldn't have ordinarily known this information about the person; it was revealed by God.

For example, you might know their street address or their children's names through a word of knowledge, which could strongly impact a person. A more general word might be that they are patient, and it takes a lot for their patience to be worn down. Another word might be that they are very caring, and they've often given their last dollar to someone in need.

Words of knowledge about character traits are very touching, and they let people know that God knows who they are. A word of knowledge is supernatural information about a person's past or present. Words of knowledge receive a lot of attention because you know right away if they are correct.

The gift of prophecy, however, addresses a person's future. You can say eloquent things in a prophecy about a person, and the person might not have a clue if it is right. The person might not be able to discern if it's the truth. The prophecy might relate to a dream. If you're talking about what they will do in the future, they might not have any way of discerning whether the prophecy was accurate because it refers to a future event.

But a word of knowledge is completely different because you know right away if a word of knowledge is wrong. I always like to prophesy and use a number of words of knowledge in the prophecy to emphasize and bring home the prophecy and show the person that God truly knows what he is talking about.

Words of wisdom are directional words of how to apply the knowledge that you've discerned about a person. If you've discerned that the person is gifted and called to be a prophet, words of wisdom might be that the Lord wants them to spend quite a bit of time studying the Word of God to prepare them to preach in the future and to establish a solid foundation in the Word.

A word of wisdom provides direction. God used words of wisdom all the way through the Old Testament, telling kings how to fight battles and how to accomplish what he wanted them to do.

The prominent online training school on the prophetic steered their students away from and discouraged them from giving words of wisdom to people for fear of possibly misdirecting people. The school seemed to believe that these students weren't mature enough to give words of wisdom. I was against their methods and had a falling out with that prophetic training school simply because words of wisdom should accompany the gift of prophecy. When you receive the gift of prophecy, all three gifts start to move together in your life.

If you have to edit what the Lord wants to say to a person because of rules set down by someone, then you're in serious trouble.

You are always looking to improve, and you are watching other prophets.

As a prophet, you'll flow in the gift of prophecy and look at other prophets to see their style and how they prophesy. Sometimes you can adapt their manner of prophecy and gain understanding into the prophetic by watching different prophets.

You can be encouraged by watching an experienced prophet, but you might be intimidated as well. In either case, you will learn so much by watching someone who's more experienced than you. It won't hurt you to watch someone who's very proficient at the gift, but it will help strengthen your gift.

You may consume many books on the prophetic.

One reason that you bought this book is because you're interested in learning more about the prophetic. This book was written for you. If you're enjoying this book, I'm very happy because it was written for people like you.

If you're called to be a prophet, you're always learning more from
- the Bible,
- YouTube videos,
- sermons,
- articles,
- blog posts,
- books,
- Facebook groups,
- And from like-minded people discussing and talking about the prophetic.

You are always learning more.

As a prophet, I have never stopped pursuing knowledge. I have a thirst to always want to consume more. The need to know more never stops or abates. If you have a calling on your life as a prophet, you too will be constantly learning more as the opportunity arises.

Just yesterday, I signed up for an online course with Shawn Bolz, a noted American prophet. The Holy Spirit put it on my heart to sign up for the course, and he kept on reminding me until I actually signed up and paid.

Why would I sign up to take a course when I have written thirty-eight books, and I am already a prophet? Because the calling of a prophet is a life of learning.

Sign 14:
You are spiritually hungry.

If you are called to be a prophet, you will probably be spiritually hungry. You are like a person who has walked through a desert and come to an oasis—thirsty for water and hungry for something to eat. You are in a spiritual state as a prophetic person.

Tonight I went out with a couple of spiritually hungry men who are learning to walk in the prophetic from me. I have met them twice, and they are full of questions.

You have hundreds of questions about the faith and your role.

When you're spiritually hungry, you'll have hundreds of questions about Bible verses. You'll want to know about hundreds of things, and you'll always be on the lookout to learn more. You'll read books, watch videos, and listen to sermons. You'll do everything you can to learn the answers to the questions, and you'll be especially interested in the role of a prophet. You will have your ears open to find out more about the role of a prophet.

You will learn so much from reading books because you really want to know what the prophet's role is and what the prophetic is all about. The more you learn, the more experienced you become.

Every time a question is answered, more questions come up.

Sometimes you can learn an answer to a major question, such as when Jesus says that he will say one day to people, "Depart from me, I never knew you" (Matthew 7:23).

You have asked yourself, "What does that mean?"

Someone can answer that question. They might say, "Yes, some people are anointed and have the gifts of the Spirit and operate in them, but they have become lustful or money hungry and idolatrous, and they fall away. Jesus will say to them in those days, 'Depart from me, I never knew you.'"

Once that question is answered, more questions come up, such as the following:
- How to prevent falling away,
- What it means to have too much lust,
- What position is going after too much money, and
- How to stop money from becoming your idol in ministry.

You have many more questions because you are hungry.

Your whole life is consumed with the knowledge of God.

If you're called as a prophet, your whole life is probably filled up and consumed as you pursue the knowledge of God. Everything about the Bible interests and fascinates you except for possibly Leviticus and Numbers.

The Bible interests you. You spend so much of your time reading the Bible and reading books about God's Word. You want to learn everything that you can about the Christian faith. You want answers to your questions, and just as they are answered, more questions surface. As I said, you'll always have questions when you're spiritually hungry.

The more you learn, the more excited and the hungrier you'll become.

You'll never reach a stage where you know it all. Some people who are quite religious and strict think they know the meaning of every verse and think they know it all. But as you pursue God and pursue the things of God to become a prophet, the more you will learn, the more excited you will become, and the hungrier you will become.

I've been hearing the word reformation spread around. I'd like to know what kind of reformation people believe that God will bring to the church. I am hungry to learn what the apostles are talking about and what they really think. What I've learned personally from the Bible, Jesus, and my intimacy with him is that the church is blind and full of blind shepherds leading the blind.

I have become hungry for the answers and very interested in reformation when it comes to totally replacing the structures and the teachings of men. I'm hungry for this.

The people in heaven never stop their learning. People move from one glory to the next as weeks go by in earth time. They are constantly learning, moving, and growing in heaven. Why shouldn't we move, grow, and prosper in the kingdom on earth if they're already doing it in heaven? If they're constantly growing in heaven, then there's always room for growth for us on earth.

Sign 15:
You hate sin.

You have grace for sinners, but you don't like sin.

The godlier you become, the closer to God you become, the more you are filled with love and compassion. You have an ability to deal with people who are steeped in sin, involved in a sinful lifestyle, or dealing with a habit that you don't like. You don't like the ways or the traps of the enemy. You don't like how the enemy holds people in bondage and punishes them and puts them through trials and to the test.

The humbler that you become, the more you can't stand the sin of pride. The more loving you become, the more resistant you are to hate, slander, and gossip. The more loving you become, the more you dislike all of the different sins that hold people in bondage.

One of your roles as a prophet is to teach people to crucify their flesh and how to be reborn into the new man. You teach people how to be led by the Spirit and how to depend on the grace and provision of the Spirit to overcome sin in their personal lives. You teach people how to live a holy and set-apart life.

Part of your skill set is to show people how to develop such an intimate relationship with Jesus so that sin just falls away and off people like scales coming off a fish. Sin falls off like sand running off your beach towel as you pick up the towel and shake it so that all the sand comes out. You are full of love and grace for sinners, but you certainly have a message of repentance. You have a message that will help people confess and turn away from their sins.

You're not going to preach a message that everything is okay or fine or that God loves you no matter what you do. You'll preach a message that talks about turning away from worldly lust and the sins of the flesh and turning to Jesus and being renewed by the Holy Spirit and his power, love, and his compassion for you.

Your posts on social media sometimes address sin.

In Australia, people voted to introduce gay marriage in 2017. The Australian public filled out a survey asking for its legalization. In the course of that happening, many Christian people I knew in the gay community put pressure on others not to speak out against gay marriage.

During that season, my posts on Facebook made it clear that I was a prophet and standing on the covenant of marriage between one man and a wife. The man should leave his mother and father, cleave to his wife, and the two shall become one. (See Ephesians 5:31.) They saw that I didn't condone gay marriage. I don't think it's acceptable; I don't think God sees gay marriage as a true union in his sight. Although the Australian government allows them to be married, the homosexual act is still a sin.

As a prophet, you'll speak out about sin. You won't be afraid to be politically incorrect and go against the tide of evil sweeping our nations.

You are very aware of sin in your own life.

If you have any sin in your own life, you are very aware of it. You're in the process of trying to conquer the sin and get over it and live a grace-enabled life so that you can live without sinning. You don't boast about sin. You don't dismiss it or think that you can get away with it forever because it's all covered under the grace of God. You're aware of it and working toward walking in holiness.

As a prophet, you love people, but you love them enough to correct them and point them in the right direction when the lifestyle or what they are doing is contradicting or coming against the clear teachings in the Bible.

Sign 16:
You don't like to hear error taught.

It annoys you to hear error taught.

Some prevalent errors are being taught in the Body of Christ. The grace camp teaches many errors. For example, they teach that the only time you need to repent for your sins is when you're born again, and from that point on, you don't have to confess your sins to God because you're already forgiven.

They say that the cross paid the price for all your past, current, and future sins, so you don't have to worry about repentance to have your sins forgiven.

They say that you don't have to do any works in the kingdom of God. They say that obeying the commands of Jesus and doing what he taught is a form of works and is not living the grace-filled life. They think that the grace-filled life is a life of no works. So they teach that you don't have to obey Jesus's teachings.

Jesus himself said that anyone that teaches people to disobey his commandments will be considered the least in the kingdom of God. (See Matthew 5:19.) Jesus said at the end of Matthew, in the Great Commission (Matthew 28:16–20), "Teaching them to obey everything that I commanded you." Jesus said after the Resurrection that the disciples should teach the new converts to obey everything that he taught them.

Many grace teachers will teach that everything before the Resurrection was the law and Jesus was preaching the law. Then grace came in after the Resurrection. They don't obey the teachings of Jesus, and they feel that Jesus was teaching the law.

Other error says how can a loving God send people to eternal damnation? How can a loving God send people to hell? They insist that if you look at the Greek and if you study it as they do and if you learn what they have learned, you'll know that there is no hell and that God doesn't send people to hell. They teach that everyone, including the angels and Satan, will be safe in the end. Everyone will bow before Jesus one day and give their lives to him. No one can resist Jesus forever.

The lie that there is no hell and that everyone will eventually go to heaven is an error. As a prophet, when you see error like that taught, it frustrates and upsets you. As you mature in your gifting, you'll be able to build arguments that clearly spell out error. You'll be able to show people what the real truth is.

You try to correct error with grace and humility when you can.

If someone posts one of these errors that I've mentioned or other errors on their Facebook wall, you can try and correct the error with grace and humility if you have a solid relationship with that person.

I have to strongly impress upon you that you are to correct people with grace in love and with humility. It's biblical to correct people with humility. As an emerging prophet, you'll be called by the Holy Spirit to correct the error of your friends from time to time.

You have learned the truth and are a vocal preacher of truth and exposing the error you used to embrace.

I used to be legalistic and believe that God was an angry God. I've read the Old Testament prophets forty times, and I truly believed in the painful and angry God. I had to have my ideas about God transformed. I was convinced of the grace message, but I swung the pendulum too far the other way. I realized that I'd gone into a camp that was also full of error.

So I swung the pendulum back to the middle where grace people think that I'm a bit legalistic and legalistic people think that I'm a greasy-grace preacher. I sit firmly in the middle now. As you emerge as a prophet, you'll learn the truth so that you're a vocal preacher of that truth. You expose error and teach people about the error that you used to believe.

You understand that people need to know the truth.

If you're called as a prophet, you understand that people need to know the truth. When you're given a platform, you share the truth that you're learning, the truth that you're being led to by the Holy Spirit. You share that truth with the people in your circle of influence.

You know that when you have a bigger platform, you will do more in this area.

You know the truth and what error is. You know the errors that are being taught, and you know the truth from the lies. As God promotes you, you'll have more Facebook friends. You will start to receive invitations to churches to preach. As God opens doors and as your profile expands and as you have a bigger platform and as God starts to use you, you will continue to preach these same truths.

So much of the prophetic journey is waiting for open doors and waiting for God to use you. I said before that you could start to share your revelations and your teaching on YouTube. You can start with this platform before you become successful and before you are used mightily by God.

Sign 17:
You deal with lots of warfare.

Your past might have had lots of abuse and warfare where Satan tried to derail you.

If you are called to be a prophet, if you are called to be used in a significant way for the Lord to preach the gospel to do the works of the kingdom in the future, Satan will often try to derail you. He'll try to shift your course. He'll try to sabotage the gifting that's within you and your future.

Like me, you might have been sexually molested or struggled with an addiction to prostitutes and an addiction to pornography. He'll try and totally destroy your life to stop you from ever recovering or from ever getting into a position where you can claim to be a sober, righteous preacher of the gospel.

Twenty years ago, I reviewed my life and found that my life could have ended about thirteen times. I almost died thirteen times. Since then, I have had a few more close encounters with death. As you can tell from the number of times that I could have died, the warfare is intense in my life.

You can tell that there's a strong calling on your life when the enemy has tried really hard to sabotage your future and to stop you from being a righteous, holy, devoted preacher of the gospel.

You struggle with a lot of warfare through people that come against you.

If you're called to the office of prophet, you might find that people come against you for no apparent reason. You can just be minding your own business at work when someone hates you for seemingly no reason and starts to speak out against you. They might start to gossip about you and say negative things about you to others. They might complain to the boss about you or do things to make your life uncomfortable.

This is sometimes the result of an evil spirit in them hating the righteousness, hating the pure spirit, that's within you. Some of that warfare is an agent of Satan in those people coming against you because you're a righteous son of God. When you face that kind of warfare from people you don't know who have no apparent reason for coming against you, you can see evidence that you have a calling on your life and that Satan definitely hates you.

Satan doesn't often come down to manifest in the flesh or to visit you in a vision to frighten and hurt you, though it can happen. Many times, Satan uses demons in the lives of other people to come against you.

Remember, we do not fight against flesh and blood but against principalities and powers. (See Ephesians 6:10–18.)

Satan certainly hates emerging prophets. Your life could have been rocky with many people coming against you if you have a prophetic calling on your life.

Jezebel might come against you many times.

As a prophet, I've experienced Jezebel influencing my life and coming against me many times. Many women and men with the Jezebel spirit have tried to become close to me and befriend me to try and influence me and move against me.

The Jezebel spirit hates being identified. Read the book by Bill Vincent, *Destroying the Jezebel Spirit: How to Overcome the Spirit Before It Destroys You!*

This book provides you with information about the character traits of the Jezebel spirit so that when you discern these traits, you'll be able to avoid the influence of people with the Jezebel spirit. You'll be able to quickly discern them so that they leave you and stop affecting your life.

You can go from one hard situation to the next more often than other people.

No matter if you're called to be a prophet or not, people seem to go from one crisis to the next. But someone with a big calling on their life will face many more difficulties, with more troubles, with more trials, and with more stresses.

A close friend of mine, Laura, has been going through tribulations for about five years. She's been in this fire of the Lord and has been attacked from all angles. She's suffered financial difficulties, homelessness, and was almost being trafficked in the sex trade. She's faced all sorts of difficult situations. She seems to be in the midst of this terrible, terrible life. She has a calling as a prophet on her life. These problems are not all her doing and not due to her bad choices. You might suffer in the same way if you are called as a prophet.

Sign 18:
You have a fire in your belly.

Jeremiah is famous for saying that he had a fire in his belly, and he was weary of keeping it in. (See Jeremiah 20:9.)

You have a message of change for your local church.

If you're called as a prophet, you might be in a church where you're not acknowledged or recognized as an emerging prophet.

In the early years of your development, it might be best just to call yourself prophetic rather than calling yourself a prophet. As your gift starts to emerge and as you start to increase in discernment, you will receive more revelation from the Lord in scripture and in your spirit. You will know things about your local church that need to change.

You might have a clear message of change for the local church that you attend. That can become a burden on your heart that you want to share with the pastor. You might want to go into the pulpit and preach that message. But if your pastor doesn't recognize that you have the gift to preach or recognize you as a prophet, he might never call you to preach that message.

You might try and engage your pastor in conversations and share what you feel that the Lord is saying. He may not have the time, the concern, or the desire to listen to your thoughts. Even so, you might have a fire in your belly.

I've attended a church where I had a message to share, but I wasn't allowed to share it. The pastor recognized me as a prophet with the ability to prophesy over anyone in the church. I had the freedom from the pastor to prophesy over people. Although they recognized me as a prophet, they didn't extend the invitation to me to preach in the church.

As a prophet, you think that you have the answer for your church or a message for them. You should not bring a strong message of repentance if the pastor hasn't released you to do so. That message might come from a visiting prophet who's been released by the pastor to preach a message that would bring change and repentance to the church.

A visiting preacher might preach the message that you want to preach. Nonetheless, you might still have the burden on your spirit, which is the fire in your belly.

Sometimes a church might refuse to let a prophet speak. If you attend a church like that, it might be wise to find a different church that is open to the prophetic.

You flow and preach from the new wine.

You have a message of change for the Body of Christ. You have the new wine and a new message that the church needs to hear, to understand, and to put into practice in their lives. Sometimes the church is full of the blind leading the blind. You have a message that will illuminate the path: a path to victory, to change, and to empowerment.

That message might burn in your heart, but you won't receive many invitations to speak in churches. When you're waiting to be released into your prophetic office, you might not have many opportunities to share that message. Instead, share the message on YouTube even if you only have fifty followers.

I know from personal experience that it can be frustrating to have a burden on your heart for the Body of Christ but no platform to speak. That burden can lead to the depression that we were talking about earlier.

You need to preach a message of love, purity, and holiness.

You might have a message of love, purity, and holiness that you want to share with the church. You want to share how to live a life that's consecrated and totally set apart for God and not the things of world. You have a message about keeping your heart pure before God. You want to speak on how to be holy, devoted, and in passionate pursuit of God.

You have a message of intimacy to show the Body of Christ how to live a life of love for God and how to have a rewarding relationship with Jesus Christ. You have this burden on your heart to preach to your local church or to any church that will invite you to preach.

While you have a burden to preach, you might be held back. God in his wisdom doesn't release you to preach until the appointed time.

You want the church to wake up and to stop being lukewarm.

In the book of Revelation, Jesus calls one of the churches lukewarm. He says that they are not passionate; they are not hot or cold, like a witch or an atheist, but they're in the middle, lukewarm. If you've tried to drink a cup of lukewarm coffee or if you've taken a bath in lukewarm water, neither of these is pleasant. The lukewarm coffee and meal are terrible, and the lukewarm bath is unpleasant.

The state of the Western church is now lukewarm. You might have a message to preach to the church. If you could write a best-selling book with your message, you would see great changes.

You want the platform so that you can share this burden from your heart.

You might have a burden to preach on all these things, but you need a platform to preach from to release this burden from your heart. You want that platform, and as a prophet, you just have to wait until the Lord opens those doors for you.

Between now and when the platform opens up and when the invitations come in, the Lord Jesus will do some very important work in your life.

Sign 19:
You live a supernatural life filled with visions, dreams, and angels.

You hear the Godhead speak to you.

As an emerging prophet, you can speak to God the Father, to Jesus, and to the Holy Spirit, and you can hear the Trinity speak to you.

You also can develop the ability to discern the difference between each of their voices. Instead of the Father saying "This is the Father speaking," and then saying something to you, you know immediately when the Father is speaking. You don't have to ask if it's the Father.

Very few people in the church know how to hear all three persons in the Godhead speak to them. In my estimation, only about 20 percent of the church can hear Jesus speak to them. In the parable of the good shepherd, Jesus says, "My sheep hear my voice. I call them up by name and they follow me." (See John 10:27–30.)

If you consider yourself one of Jesus's sheep or one of his followers, then you should be able to hear his voice. If you can hear Jesus's voice, then you can quickly learn to discern the Father's voice and the voice of the Holy Spirit.

Two books that might help you in this area are:
- *Hearing God's Voice Made Simple (The Kingdom of God Made Simple Book 3)* by Praying Medic and

- _How to Hear God's Voice: Keys to Conversational Two-Way Prayer_.

You have the ability to see in the Spirit.

Many people think that it's trendy to call themselves seers these days. In the Old Testament, a prophet that could see in the Spirit was called a seer, but many people with the gift of seeing in the Spirit are calling themselves seers these days, which is a bit confusing.

If you're called as a prophet, you might have the ability to see in the Spirit, including visions of angels and visions of Jesus. You'll be able to see visions that God gave you or visions of the future. You'll be able to imagine a location in another country in your mind and then go there in the Spirit. This is also called translating in the Spirit. Emerging prophets sometimes can see in the Spirit.

Two books that might help you develop in this area are:
- _Seeing in the Spirit Made Simple (The Kingdom of God Made Simple Book 2)_ by Praying Medic and
- _How to See in the Spirit: A Practical Guide on Engaging the Spirit Realm_ by Michael Van Vlymen.

You have prophetic dreams.

God will allow a seer, someone who can see in the Spirit, to be driven and directed by dreams and visions. Prophetic dreams are often a part of a prophet's life. As part of the supernatural life, God often gives you prophetic messages through your dreams. You can have dreams and learn to interpret them. Experienced prophets can interpret your dreams for you. Other people with the gift of interpretation of dreams can also interpret the dreams for you.

You'll find that some of your dreams will give you direction, just like other prophetic words that you receive.

I recently planned to write a controversial book. Jesus gave me a dream although I rarely have prophetic dreams. The interpretation of the dream was that it would be spiritual suicide for me to produce that controversial book. I canceled my plans to write it even though I had already spent a lot of money on it. I stopped the whole process of the book. Prophetic dreams can be very important and useful.

You may see angels.

My guardian angel, Michael, is also a prophetic angel and stewards my prophetic gift. Bethany, my scribe angel, helps me write posts on Facebook and helps me write books. I have talked about her before. Elisha is over my other angels. He will do more work in the future when I'm used in revival for some of the signs and wonders and other works.

Mark is my finance angel, and he puts it on people's hearts to donate to my ministry, to request a prophecy, or to simply contribute to my book-publishing ministry. Mark puts it on people's hearts to request life coaching or a message from an angel. He is very useful. Since he has been involved in my life, I have been able to meet every financial need. I produce an average of a book every month at a cost of about two thousand dollars. The money comes in for the book production with the help of Mark. I've seen my angels and talked to and interacted with them.

If you want to read more about my accounts with angels, you can check out these two books:
- <u>My Radical Encounters with Angels: Angels in the Flesh, Angels of Protection and More</u> and
- <u>My Radical Encounters with Angels—Book Two: Meeting Angels, Witches, Demons, Satan, Jesus and More!</u>

You have been to heaven.

As an emerging prophet, you have probably had a vision of heaven. You can either leave your body on earth and go to heaven in the spirit, or you can actually stay on earth and just see heaven in your mind and in your imagination.

You can be sure that when you see heaven in your mind, it's not just your imagination. It's actually an encounter of heaven. That's how I go to heaven. Today I talked to two hungry individuals and taught them more about the prophetic. I took both of them to heaven, and they encountered heaven.

If you want to read of some of my encounters in heaven, you can read <u>My Visits to Heaven: Lessons Learned</u>.

You have met Jesus.

Many songs say that it will be such a great day when we meet Jesus in heaven or talk about the day that we'll meet Jesus face to face. Many worship songs talk about that. But part of your inheritance as an emerging prophet is to have visions of Jesus and not only visit heaven and meet Jesus but have Jesus come to earth and meet you in a vision.

You know, a hymn from our childhood called "In the Garden" says that Jesus walks with me and he talks with me.[1] So you can walk and talk with Jesus like the writer of that song did.

You have met saints.

I have met different saints in the Bible, people that live in heaven, although this is a bit controversial. I've met them when they visited earth. Jesus met Moses and Elijah on the Mount of Transfiguration when he was on earth. (See Matthew 17:1–13.) Sometimes when you have an intimate relationship with Jesus, you can meet saints from heaven.

You can also meet saints on earth. As an emerging prophet, you might lead a supernatural life.

---

[1] "In the Garden (1912 Song)." *Wikipedia.* Last modified March 24, 2018, https://en.wikipedia.org/wiki/In_the_Garden_(1912_song)

You can read more about my visits with saints in my book *My Visits to the Galactic Council of Heaven: Book 1*.

Sign 20:
You develop the mind of Christ.

Through understanding Christ's teachings and obeying them, you develop the ability to think like Jesus.

John 14:21 says, "He who has My commandments and keeps them, it is he who loves Me. And he who loves Me will be loved by My Father, and I will love him and manifest Myself to him."

This verse says that if you obey Jesus, he will manifest himself to you. One understanding of what this means, a literal interpretation of that passage, is to actually meet Jesus in visions. This verse can be your pathway to visions of Jesus, giving you the authority and the ability to see him.

Another way to interpret this verse is that once you know the teachings and commandments of Jesus and start to practice them, you can show your love to Jesus and understand his personality.

If you're constantly living your life so that you're directed by what Jesus taught you, if you're constantly acting how Jesus commanded you to act as his follower, you seem to develop the mind of Christ. Your mind starts to transform and you develop the mind of Christ because you're often thinking and making decisions based on what Jesus taught. (See Romans 12:1–2.)

As an emerging prophet, you can think like Jesus.

You feel the heart of Jesus for people.

About thirty years ago, I was sharing with a person at a Christian coffee lounge. He seemed rather hardened to the gospel. But he began to open up to me, and he shared that he felt like killing himself. I could share with him that I had felt like killing myself and that Jesus had turned that around. When I admitted to him that I felt like killing myself, he opened up further.

As he opened up further, Jesus showed me what was in his heart. Jesus let me understand how he felt. I could then feel his emotions. Then Jesus changed my perspective and gave me an impression of what Jesus thought and how he felt about this guy. Both of these perspectives helped me understand the heart of Jesus for him. I could then minister the love of Jesus to him from my heart.

You know how Jesus loves a person.

In the previous example, I could feel the heart of Jesus for that person. As an emerging prophet, you can develop the ability to ask Jesus how he feels about a certain person, and Jesus will show you his heart for them. This is especially useful when you're witnessing or ministering to someone in pain.

Once you feel the heart of Jesus for a person, you can easily open up and prophesy with love because you understand his or her heart.

You start to move from knowledge of scripture to wisdom and application of the Word.

The Holy Spirit told me ten years ago that wisdom is the proper application of knowledge. A lot of knowledge is in the world, but very few people walk in wisdom. James talks about asking for wisdom in James 1:5–8. "If any of you lacks wisdom, let him ask of God, who gives to all liberally and without reproach, and it will be given to him. But let him ask in faith, with no doubting, for he who doubts is like a wave of the sea driven and tossed by the wind. For let not that man suppose that he will receive anything from the Lord; he is a double-minded man, unstable in all his ways."

Many people see this scripture and ask for wisdom when wisdom is the proper application of knowledge. Many people know scriptures but aren't actively applying those scriptures in their lives. When you start to apply the scriptures in your life, you will walk in wisdom, which is the mind of Christ. You start to walk in the very mind of Christ and act like Jesus.

Three people have said that I am the most Christlike person they have ever met. These people were very loved by me and knew me well. They also know many other Christians. Hundreds of readers might think the same of me.

So you move from your knowledge of the scripture to wisdom, which is actual application of the scripture.

You take every thought captive and pull down thoughts that don't agree with the Word of God.

Scripture tells us to take every thought captive in 2 Corinthians 10:4–6.

People sometimes struggle with how to take thoughts captive. You do this by understanding everything that's taught in the New Testament, including the commands of Jesus.

When a thought comes to your mind and demands that you take action, you apply all the scriptures to that thought and then decide what to do with that thought. If the thought is telling you to contradict or disobey a scripture, then you don't do what the thought is telling you to do.

Scripture talks about gossip, slander, hate, envy, and jealousy. If you have thoughts of slandering a person due to jealousy, scripture tells you not to slander but to love your enemies. Scripture says don't pay a person back, but if your enemy offends you, you feed them and give them water. (See Romans 12:17 and 1 Peter 3:9.) Instead of hurting the person, do them a favor. Bless your enemy. Don't curse them.

We need to make our decisions based on what scripture says to do and when you do that, you're taking every thought captive. That's how you move or act with the mind of Christ.

As an emerging prophet, you will learn to walk and act with the mind of Christ.

Sign 21:
You have God's heart.

You have a sense of how God feels.

I've had conversations with God. I have three books with conversations with God so that you can have a better idea of God and his heart: <u>Conversations with God: Book 1</u>, <u>Conversations with God: Book 2</u>, and <u>Conversations with God: Book 3</u>. If you click on any one of these links, you can order the Kindle version of my books for ninety-nine cents.

You can have a sense of God's heart through your own conversations with him and hear him speak. As an emerging prophet, you can feel God's heart for a person or for a situation. For example, I was watching the news when something came on about child sex abusers. The news talked about an upcoming special investigation into pedophilia in the church, and I sensed that God was grieved and his heart was broken.

When I pressed him on the grief in his heart, I felt his heart for the situation. I then asked God, "Why are you upset?"

God replied, "I'm upset for the victims."

I asked, "Aren't you afraid that this exposure of pedophiles will do your church a disservice?"

He replied, "Let the church look after itself. The victims will have their day in court." God was truly concerned about the victims receiving justice and having the ability to speak about the abuse they suffered.

As an emerging prophet, you have God's heart on topics. You might not have the interpretation of a certain scripture, but you actually have God's heart. Even as you read the scriptures and the Bible, you will feel God's heart about the scripture when it applies to a certain situation.

You can have the heart of God and make decisions based on that intuition and feeling.

When you have the heart of God, when you feel what God feels, you can follow that intuition and feeling and make decisions based on that.

You can have God's heart and understand how he's feeling and what he is thinking. You can look at your Facebook friends who are preaching false doctrines. You can watch and read and study their arguments and how they present these false teachings. You can develop an ability to listen and watch without commenting. You have discerned God's heart in the situation. He might just want you to observe and listen and collect information.

After some time, he might actually have you write articles or blog posts on those false teachings. For example, topics might include why there is a hell or why everyone won't be saved or why people need to obey the commands of Jesus.

But first, God's heart might be for you just to watch your friends and observe. Further down the road, his heart might be for you to write up clever arguments. Meanwhile, you continue to build relationships with all these friends that are in error. One day when they post the error, you might have the freedom to share what you've written with them. The blog post or article will expose the error and belief with love and humility.

As an emerging prophet, you can have a sense of God's heart and intuitively feel what he's feeling. I used that example because God had given me that kind of heart in certain situations. I was not released to speak out or to argue on Facebook posts but to observe and read everything and then collect information and write about it.

You love people like God does with grace and compassion.

As an emerging prophet, you can actually love people with grace and compassion like God does. Scripture says that God extends mercy to the merciful. (See James 2:13.) The Bible also says that God will punish certain people. (See Psalm 94 and Isaiah 65.) You can have a godly attitude and show people mercy, grace, and compassion. Only through knowing God can you act like him. By knowing God's heart, you can act how he wants you to act.

Sign 22:
You can be misunderstood and rejected.

Because you are so turned on to Jesus and holy living, you can be brash in your immaturity, which causes people to reject you.

As an emerging prophet, you can be rude as you try and convince others to be like you because you're so passionate about Jesus and not serving the world. You might not necessarily be rude, but some prophets are rude. This might be due to your zeal and your passion for God. You are trying to talk people into your way of understanding and thinking. We can all experience that passion, which can sometimes be misunderstood as arrogance.

People can sometimes feel embarrassed because they are not measuring up to your standards. But in that case, they might not want to be around you because they don't want to feel guilty. They might think that you're rude or brash. They don't want to be around you and don't want to be your friend.

You have this fire in your belly, and you want to preach. In your passion, you can mistakenly share your revelations and message with one of your friends. They don't have the same revelation or that fire in their belly. They don't have the calling that you have. They don't see the problem with the church. They might think that you are being condescending or judgmental to the church. They believe that you think you're better than the pastor and the church leadership. They might see pride in you.

They might see all those things, but they might not be right. You might be humble; you might not think you're better than the pastor. But what they see is what they see. As such, they will reject you and misunderstand the message you carry.

You are different. Because you have unique revelation that differs from what has been traditionally taught, you are misunderstood and rejected.

Passionate people and emerging prophets often make the common mistake of sharing revelation with their friends. But their friends aren't prophets. They don't have a calling on their lives. They are just ordinary Christians. They are not receiving the same revelation as you. If you receive revelation that is different, controversial, or unusual, people might not believe your revelation.

You might be excited that God is saying something new. You might feel that God is moving in a new way. But if other prophets and teachers have not shared that revelation, you will be misunderstood and rejected.

Sadly, your passion—the burden on your heart and the message in your belly that's burning like a fire—can get you into trouble. Many young prophets and those in training have an issue with pride and think they are receiving special revelation. They'll hear the message and say things like:

- I know what's wrong with the church.
- People need to stop serving the world and start serving God.
- People need to stop being lukewarm.
- The church needs to stop letting the blind lead the blind.
- I have all the revelation.
- I have all the understanding.
- The church should listen to me.

Well, the church should not listen to you. You're just someone in the congregation that can prophesy from time to time. You don't have experience or a Bible college degree. You're not a church pastor or in a position of authority. What credentials do you have? Who are you to be speaking like that? Who do you think you are?

That's what they'll think about you and how they will feel. You can easily be misunderstood and rejected.

You can feel like a square peg in a round hole.

I went out with some people today that are hungry for the supernatural. I'm teaching them the prophetic. They are from one of the first churches where I have been called to work. They asked me today, "How do you continue to go to church at the Salvation Army? You know, it seems dead. They are not into the supernatural or the gifts of the Spirit. Why do you keep going there?"

I answered that I continue to go there because they loved me. But I honestly feel like a square peg in a round hole at my current church. I don't fit in. People have nine to five jobs there and come to church. They are happy with a two-hour service and a half-hour sermon. They focus on work from Monday to Saturday and attend church on Sunday. On Sunday, they transform into someone spiritual. But they live their whole lives carnally the rest of the week.

I can't live like that. Jesus talks to me every day. I receive daily revelation. Every day, he appears to me. I speak daily to saints from heaven and interact with angels. I'm led by the Spirit every day. My life isn't boring.

I recorded this book in twenty-four hours. The first draft of this book will be transcribed and typed up and finished within a month. My life is different. It's hard to talk to ordinary Christians and to interact with them when you're unique.

When you're different, you can feel misunderstood and rejected. Others simply don't understand how you operate. They don't know how to accept you for who you are.

People that are closest to you might not accept that you are called to be a prophet.

Some of your closest friends might not accept that you're called to be a prophet. Others might take years or even decades to accept your call. Still others might never accept it. Your closest friends might be Facebook friends and strangers. You might be very lonely. In due time, you will find others like you, other square pegs in round holes, those who are called as prophets who are different and passionate like you.

God is doing a move in this world and connecting the dots. He is connecting people together to build relationships and to start to minister with each other.

The call to be a prophet takes fifteen to twenty years to develop. If you allow it to, this season of misunderstanding and rejection will mature you into a great prophet.

The calling of a prophet can take fifteen to twenty years to mature. All of the misunderstanding or rejection will teach, humble, purify, and transform you into a seasoned prophet one day.

You can read my other books to learn more about the prophetic office, including:

- *The Prophetic Supernatural Experience,*
- *Deep Calls unto Deep,*
- *A Beginner's Guide to the Prophetic,* and
- *Prophetic Evangelism Made Simple.*

Closing Thoughts

Do any of these signs describe you? Do you feel as if you might be called as a prophet? Have prophetic people told you that you're called as a prophet? Do you understand the prophetic books in the Bible? Do you relate to other prophets?

Do these signs line up with what you are feeling? If you can identify with fifteen to twenty of these signs, you might be called as a prophet, especially if established prophets have prophesied over you. If you have not yet received prophecies about your calling, keep going. Keep pressing into Jesus and see what happens.

You know, Jesus doesn't make mistakes. He made you a passionate, zealous, and happy Christian who wants everything that the Lord has for him or her. You might have many of these characteristics and just be a passionate Christian who God will use to contend with evil.

You might be an evangelist, or you might carry a healing anointing and a prophetic gift. You might just be an ordinary person and not called as a prophet. This book is titled this way so that you can investigate these points. You can consider if God has called you as a prophet.

I wrote this book after I posted about this subject on Facebook. A lot of people responded to the post, so I decided to write a book about it. I made a ten-minute video about it, and I was impressed to speak about each point for about thirty to sixty seconds. It really impressed me. I thought that I should make a book about this. But I wondered how I could speak ten minutes on each point when I couldn't even last thirty seconds on each point.

The Holy Spirit told me to make a bullet list of points under each main heading and then just spend two minutes on each of those sub-topics. I was led by the Holy Spirit to go through each of the twenty-two main topics and then talk about each sub-topic. I then printed out the list and used that list to dictate this book.

I have dictated this book from the headings and from each bullet point. I did not do any research for this book or plan it. All I had was the main headings and the sub-headings in an hour. This book has been spoken from my own experience as a prophet over the last twenty years.

I've made many mistakes. I've been brash, frightful, and made mistakes in prophecy. I've conducted myself unwisely. I've argued with people on Facebook. I've done all sorts of different things that you shouldn't do. I say weird things. I still make people shake their heads and wonder what kind of person I am. But I am true to myself.

I love the Lord with all of my heart. I don't have to be anyone special. I don't have to be the chief apostle or the chief prophet in charge of Australia. I'm happy to follow the Lord wherever he takes me and to go through doors as he opens them for me to minister.

At present, I've spoken in churches four times, and about twelve hundred people read my books each month. This will be the fortieth book that I've written. I'm teaching the Body of Christ and fulfilling my prophetic role even though I haven't worked in many churches.

As of the writing of this book, I'm working with my first church and teaching the people there to walk in the prophetic and use their gift in prophetic evangelism to witness at their Friday night outreach. I'm in my second week of training and hope to be with them for at least six months. I hope to make their church my home church.

I'm still learning, but I have a lot of knowledge and certainly have burdens on my heart to touch the world and to teach others. I want to share the wonderful mysteries of the kingdom of God with everyone. I am burdened to change the lukewarm church and to show the blind teachers their error. I want to correct error. I have many things that I want to do and achieve.

But my purpose in writing this book and in spending the two thousand dollars to produce this book and then sell it for ninety-nine cents is to encourage you whether you are called as a prophet or just as a passionate believer. I want to encourage you to press on to the measure and the high calling of God for your life. Being passionate for Jesus is still significant even if you aren't called as a prophet.

If many of these points fit you but you still don't feel called as a prophet, you're still absolutely beautiful and created with a purpose. I've written a book called *Finding Your Purpose in Christ*. I encourage you to read it. You can also read *Influencing Your World for Christ* if you don't think you're a prophet. I hope that those two books will help you move on and progress with your Christian life.

It's been a real honor to share with you and speak to you. I hope that you will write to me or write a review on Amazon. Let me know that this book has encouraged you. I love to hear from my readers. May God bless you in your journey.

I'd love to hear from you

One of the ways that you can bless me as a writer is by writing an honest and candid review of my book on Amazon. I always read the reviews of my books, and I would love to hear what you have to say about this one.

Before I buy a book, I read the reviews first. You can make an informed decision about a book when you have read enough honest reviews from readers. One way to help me sell this book and to give me positive feedback is by writing a review for me. It doesn't cost you a thing but helps me and the future readers of this book enormously.

To read my blog, request a life-coaching session, request your own personal prophecy, request a visit to heaven, or to receive a personal message from your angel, you can also visit my website at http://personal-prophecy-today.com All of the funds raised through my ministry website will go toward the books that I write and self-publish.

To write to me about this book or to share any other thoughts, please feel free to contact me at my personal email address at survivors.sanctuary@gmail.com

You can also friend request me on Facebook at Matthew Robert Payne. Please send me a message if we have no friends in common as a lot of scammers now send me friend requests.

You can also do me a huge favor and share this book on Facebook as a recommended book to read. This will help me and other readers.

How to Sponsor a Book Project

If you have been blessed by this book, you might consider sponsoring a book for me. It normally costs me between fifteen hundred and two thousand dollars or more to produce each book that I write, depending on the length of the book.

If you seek the Holy Spirit about financing a book for me, I know that the Lord would be eternally grateful to you. Consider how much this book has blessed you and then think of hundreds or even thousands of people who would be blessed by a book of mine. As you are probably aware, the vast majority of my books are ninety-nine cents on Kindle, which proves to you that book writing is indeed a ministry for me and not a money-making venture. I would be very happy if you supported me in this.

If you have any questions for me or if you want to know what projects I am currently working on that your money might finance, you can write to me at survivors.sanctuary@gmail.com and ask me for more information. I would be pleased to give you more details about my projects.

You can sow any amount to my ministry by simply sending me money via the PayPal link at this address: http://personal-prophecy-today.com/support-my-ministry/

You can be sure that your support, no matter the amount, will be used for the publishing of helpful Christian books for people to read.

Other Books by Matthew Robert Payne

The Prophetic Supernatural Experience

Prophetic Evangelism Made Simple

Your Identity in Christ

His Redeeming Love: A Memoir

Writing and Self-Publishing Christian Nonfiction

Coping with your Pain and Suffering

Living for Eternity

Jesus Speaking Today

Great Cloud of Witnesses Speak

My Radical Encounters with Angels

Finding Intimacy with Jesus Made Simple

My Radical Encounters with Angels: Book Two

A Beginner's Guide to the Prophetic

Michael Jackson Speaks from Heaven

7 Keys to Intimacy with Jesus

Conversations with God: Book 1

Optimistic Visions of Revelation

Conversations with God: Book 2

Finding Your Purpose in Christ

Influencing your World for Christ: Practical Everyday Evangelism

Deep Calls unto Deep: Answering Questions on the Prophetic

My Visits to the Galactic Council of Heaven

The Parables of Jesus Made Simple: Updated and Expanded Edition

Great Cloud of Witnesses Speak: Old and New

Walking under an Open Heaven

A Message from My Angel: Book 1

Interviews with the Two Witnesses: Enoch and Elijah Speak

Gaining Freedom from Sex Addictions: Breaking Free of Pornography and Prostitutes

Mary Magdalene Speaks from Heaven: A Divine Revelation

Princess Diana Speaks from Heaven: A Divine Revelation

How to Hear God's Voice: Keys to Conversational Two-Way Prayer

Apostle John Speaks from Heaven: A Divine Revelation

What I Believe

Great Cloud of Witnesses Speak: God's Generals

Apostle Peter Speaks from Heaven: A Divine Revelation

King David Speaks from Heaven: A Divine Revelation

You can find my published books on my Amazon author page here: http://tinyurl.com/jq3h893

Upcoming Books:

Five Keys to Successful Writing: How I Write One Book per Month

Nineteen Scriptures to Change Your Life Forever: My Life Verses

About Matthew Robert Payne

Matthew was raised in a Baptist church and was led to the Lord at the tender age of eight. He has experienced some pain and darkness in his life, which have given him a deep compassion and love for all people.

Today, he's a founding member and admin of a Facebook group called "Prophetic Training Group," and he invites you to join him there. Matthew has a commission from the Lord to train up prophets and to mentor others in the Christian faith. He does this through his Facebook posts and by writing relevant books on the Christian faith.

God has commissioned him to write at least fifty books in his life, and he spends his days writing and earning the money to self-publish. You can support him by donating money at http://personal-prophecy-today.com or by requesting any of the other services available through his ministry website.

Recently, the Lord has put it on his heart to start his own publishing company for other people's books to be called Christian Book Publishing USA. It is Matthew's hope to help some people self-publish their books in the future.

It is Matthew's prayer that this book has blessed you, and he hopes it will lead you into a deeper and more intimate relationship with God.

www.ingramcontent.com/pod-product-compliance
Lightning Source LLC
Chambersburg PA
CBHW052108070526
44584CB00017B/2385